A First Look at Dragons

by Emma Carlson-Berne

BUMBA BOOKS™

LERNER PUBLICATIONS ◆ MINNEAPOLIS

Note to Educators

Throughout this book, you'll find critical-thinking questions. These can be used to engage young readers in thinking critically about the topic and in using the text and photos to do so.

Lerner Publications Company
An imprint of Lerner Publishing Group, Inc.
241 First Avenue North
Minneapolis, MN 55401 USA

For reading levels and more information, look up this title at www.lernerbooks.com.

Main body text set in Helvetica Textbook Com Roman.
Typeface provided by Linotype AG.

Editor: Andrea Nelson **Designer:** Lauren Cooper
Lerner team: Martha Kranes

Library of Congress Cataloging-in-Publication Data

Names: Carlson-Berne, Emma, author. | Bumba Books. | Lerner Publications Company.
Title: A first look at dragons / by Emma Carlson-Berne.
Other titles: Dragons
Description: Minneapolis : Lerner Publications, 2021. | Series: Bumba Books — Fantastic creatures | Includes bibliographical references and index. | Audience: Ages 4–7 years | Audience: Grades K–1 | Summary: "Stories about dragons are found around the world. With carefully leveled text and close text-to-image match, emergent readers will love this introduction to dragons."— Provided by publisher.
Identifiers: LCCN 2019039993 (print) | LCCN 2019039994 (ebook) | ISBN 9781541596863 (Library Binding) | ISBN 9781541599727 (eBook)
Subjects: LCSH: Dragons. | Dragons—Juvenile literature.
Classification: LCC GR830.D7 B476 2020 (print) | LCC GR830.D7 (ebook) | DDC 398.24/54—dc23

LC record available at https://lccn.loc.gov/2019039993
LC ebook record available at https://lccn.loc.gov/2019039994

Manufactured in the United States of America
1-47792-48232-11/6/2019

Table of Contents

Dragons!

Picture a reptile as big as a house.

It has wings. It breathes fire!

Dragons are made-up
animals. But we can imagine
what they would be like.

Dragons might look like giant snakes or lizards. They could have scales. They might be green, black, or gold.

What other colors do you think a dragon might be?

Dragons are powerful.
They can be evil. Or
they might use their
powers to help people.

A dragon may bring

rain to dry places.

What other powers might a dragon have?

13

Dragons could live in the ocean. Or they might live in caves. They may have treasure to protect.

Long ago, people thought dragons were real. They found fossils of huge animals. They thought the fossils were dragon bones.

The fossils were not dragon bones. They were probably from dinosaurs or whales.

Dragons appear in many books and movies. It's fun to tell stories about dragons!

Parts of a Dragon

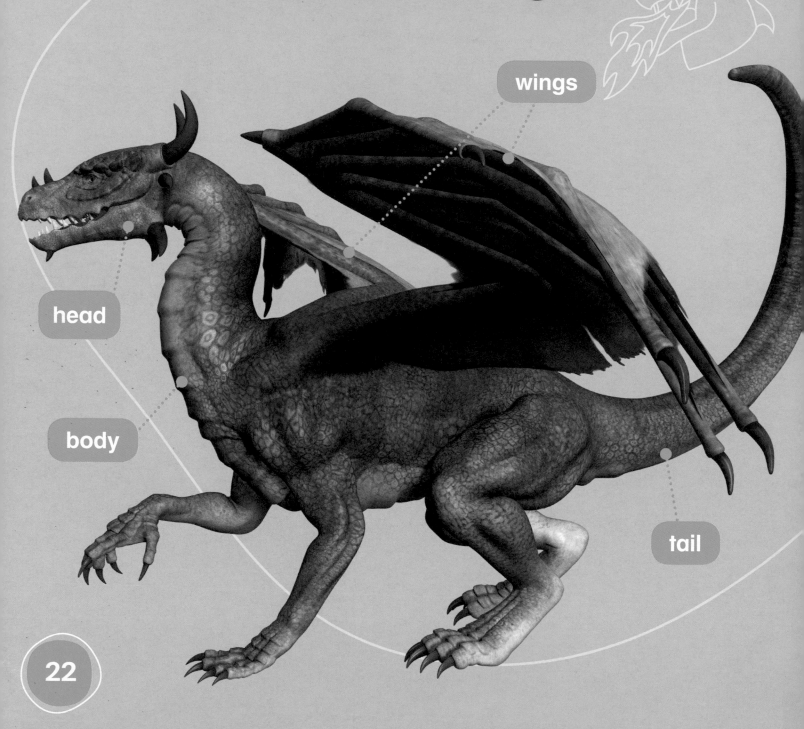

wings

head

body

tail

Picture Glossary

fossils

old animal bones that have turned to rock

reptile

an animal such as a snake or lizard that has scaly skin and lays eggs

scales

small plates that cover the bodies of some fish and reptiles

treasure

money or jewels

23

Read More

Carlson-Berne, Emma. *A First Look at Trolls*. Minneapolis: Lerner Publications, 2021.

Levine, Sara. *Fossil by Fossil: Comparing Dinosaur Bones*. Minneapolis: Millbrook, 2018.

Sayre, April Pulley. *Like a Lizard*. Honesdale, PA: Boyds Mills, 2019.

Index

Photo Credits